Kids in the White House

Frank Cornelious Funk

DEDICATION

To anyone willing and able to change
his or her mind

CONTENTS

1. CULTURAL AND MORAL BULLIES

Bullies. What are they? Where are they? How can we get rid of them? Well, they are in Hollywood. And Washington, DC. They are in Silicon Valley. They are in our schools and colleges where they are teaching our children. They are on TV. They are on Instagram. And Facebook. And Twitter. They are all over. They are immoral. They are not particularly intelligent. And they are tearing the United States of America apart.

They know very little history. But they think they know everything. Their judgement is poor. But that doesn't stop them from telling you how you should judge things. They have little understanding of civil society. But they will preach endlessly on how to be civil. They implore everyone to follow the science. But they have little understanding of what science is.

They want everyone to be equal, but they treat those with whom they disagree unequally. They want social justice but treat those with whom they are at odds unjustly.

There exists a core set of principles and ideas that human beings need to learn. These principles and ideas are explored in this book. One of the most important principles is that language is both a great tool for expressing thought and also a tool that can be used to distort thought. When I say distort thought, I mean introduce concepts into the mind that are illogical, unrealistic, or meaningless.

Watch what happens when you teach a child illogical, unrealistic, and meaningless things. The child engages in behaviors that are illogical, unrealistic, and meaningless. The situation is just as bad if you, as a parent, teach your children logical, realistic, and meaningful ideas and then send them off to school where they learn the exact opposite kinds of things. And are simultaneously bombarded through products and creations of Hollywood, the government, social media, and the like with illogical, unrealistic, and meaningless ideas.

One of the most important principles that needs to be learned is that things that are meaningful all share a similar structure. That structure can be broken down into two basic building blocks: **elements** and **relationships**.

It is by breaking things down into these fundamental building blocks that the human mind is able to understand the world it experiences. A child learns he or she has a mother and a father. Not every woman is his mother. And not every man is his father. A house is recognized because it has windows and doors and walls and a roof. Words like mother, father, and house, when said out loud, are just sounds. We hear such sounds, and a thought comes to mind. What makes that thought meaningful are the elements and relationships that comprise the thought.

Another fundamental principle is that reality, which is to say the real world we experience, also consists of elements and their relationships.

When something is considered true, the elements and relationships in our mind that define our concept of that something are wholly analogous to the form those elements and relationships take in that something as it exists in the real world. Of course, not every word calls to mind something that exists in the real world. But even those things that exist purely in the imagination can be thought of as consisting of elements and relationships.

One of the defining characteristics of cultural and moral bullies is that they often seek to **define** these elements and relationships for you in order to make you feel or think something about the world, whether or not those elements and relationships are actually true.

The individual who rejects such a **definition**, when it does not seem to him or her to be true, is then demonized by the cultural or moral bully.

In a society based on freedom of expression and freedom of thought, usually such a discrepancy in thought-process and conception would be worked out through even-handed discourse, where the two parties would explore the elements and relationships that apply to the concept and determine why there is disagreement.

The cultural and moral bully has no such desire to explore disagreement. The bully's desire is to have you accept his or her concept because the bully feels the concept is correct and justifiable. And, if you do not accept the bully's concept, often your character will be assassinated, or your motives will be questioned, or you will be asked not to express your thoughts because they are hurtful to someone else's feelings.

2. EQUALITY

The United States of America was founded on the principle that all individual human beings are created equal. What does this mean?

As physical specimens, individual human beings are not all equal. Some weigh 5 pounds when born; others may weigh 10 pounds. Some have red hair. Some have blond hair. Some have green eyes. Some have brown eyes. Some grow up to be tall. Some grow up to be short. Some men become bald in their thirties. Other men have a full head of hair at the age of 80.

These genetic variations can be taken, for all practical purposes, as random events. They are largely beyond an individual's control and the control of the individual's parents. They are for the most part unpredictable. When female and male genetic material combine to create a new human life, no one knows or can predict entirely and completely what the outcome will be.

In addition, human beings are born into circumstances beyond their control. We do not choose our parents. We do not choose the household into which we are born, the neighborhood, the city, the amount of money coming into the household on a daily, monthly, or annual basis, or the source of that money.

In a sense, these can be considered random variables.

So, in the beginning, all human beings are human beings, but each individual human being is also a unique instance of a human being. The fact is no two individual human beings ever live and grow in identical ways. Even identical twins, who share the same copies of genetic material, eventually assume distinct fates as they are shaped by the unique and distinct situations and opportunities that greet each of them, as well as by the situations and opportunities they attempt to make for themselves.

On the other hand, as citizens of the United States of America, each individual is to be treated the same way under its Laws and regulations. Each individual is born with rights which are taken to exist as inalienable, rights that are not even granted by the government, but deemed intrinsic to fact that the human has come existence as a living being. Each individual is also expected to act within the context of the Law and to be treated in the same way under the Law, those government-issued rules and regulations that each individual, as a citizen, assumes and accepts the responsibility to follow. These rules and regulations guide human behavior. And, in instances where it is determined that a Law has been broken, the consequences to the individual are determined through a system which, under ideal operating conditions, treats each individual by substantially the same process. That is what is meant by law and order. That is what is meant by justice.

The idea is this: each unique individual is born in the United States of

America with certain rights and, as citizens, agree to abide by a certain set of rules, which we call the Law, and the individual accepts the consequences if an individual's behavior is identified which violates any such rule.

The paradox is that, in the USA, individuals are born both equal and unequal. We are all human beings and we are all unique human individuals.

Where R = rules and regulations, and a circle represents an individual human being, the social structure of the United States of America can be seen as the sum of human activity that exists within a boundary which defines its territory. There exist individuals who are citizens within the boundary that defines the USA who learn and agree to follow the Laws of the United States of America and accept the consequences of breaking the Law.

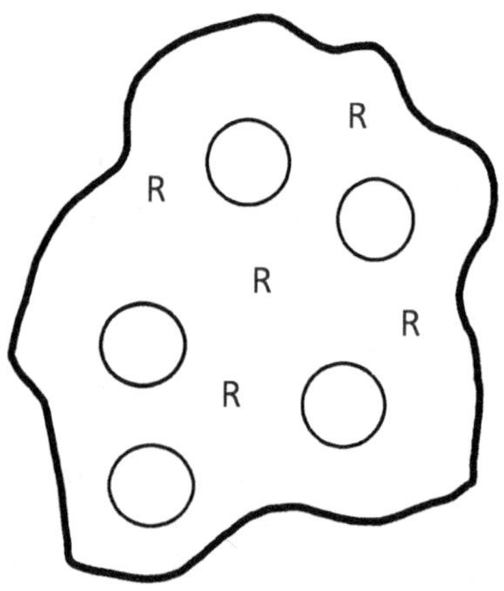

Figure 1: HUMAN SOCIAL STRUCTURE

As this diagram of human social structure (Figure 1) shows, the United States of America was not founded on the principle of slavery. It was not founded on the principle of discrimination. It was not founded on the idea that individuals can be classified into identifiable groups. It was founded on the principle that the individual human being is the primary unit of social activity and within its social structure each and every human being exists as a unique individual with defined inalienable rights who, under ideal operating conditions, is treated equally under its Laws and regulations. If such ideal conditions do not exist, it is not an indictment of these principles. It is an indictment of the imperfection of human nature.

3 PRIVATE PROPERTY

The concept of private property evolves naturally in infancy. It is inevitable that the individual human being at some time discovers that he has fingers he can move and toes he can wiggle. He has a voice and can create sounds. At some point in time, an individual human being will discover he can crawl on his knees and stand upright on his legs. He controls these things and no one else can. These body parts are integral to his being.

And no one can take his hands away. No one can take one of his legs or arms. They are his. They are parts of his body. Eventually he learns that his body itself has its own more private parts.

The feeling and thought of something being private becomes part of an individual's experience early on. It is part of the human condition. An infant at some time becomes aware that not only is his body his own, but also that it contains things that are his own. His feelings and thoughts are his and his alone to experience. His body and mind are part of the reality of being an individual human being. These things are private property.

He may get a box of wooden building blocks for his birthday and with these building blocks can build all sorts of structures. His sister may have gotten a collection of toy cars for her birthday. The toy cars are hers and his building blocks are his.

If his sister knocks down the two-foot-high skyscraper he has built with his building blocks, she has violated his space, and has destroyed something he created. If he builds a garage and takes one of his sister's toy cars and parks it in the garage he has built, he has taken something that belongs to her.

So, too, do the ideas that come to mind and feelings felt within become recognized to exist in this world of private and public things. If his sister draws a picture of a clown, and his brother likes it and decides to draw a picture of a clown, his sister might tell Mommy that he's a copycat.

Early on, the universe of social things is divided into things that are private and things that are public. The concept of private property is intrinsic to the concept of being an individual human being.

Where there exists the individual, there exists the concept of privacy. Where there exist physical things that are part of an individual's realm, there exists a universe of private things.

All living human beings exist as individuals. Where there is no conception of the human being as an individual, there is nothing that is private.

And there is a world outside of this personal and private realm which is distinct and identified as the public arena.

The distinction between private and public is intrinsic to the human condition.

Figure 2: THE INDIVIDAL HUMAN BEING

In the natural order of things, an individual from the time he is born tends to think and feel as he will, and lives with the sense that his body is his and his alone and no one is entitled to take any part of his body, control his thoughts and feelings, or take his life itself away. And each individual human being feels and thinks he or she is entitled to express what he or she thinks or feels.

4 THE RANDOM DISTRIBUTION OF WEALTH

Suppose there is something called wealth, which is of value to all individual human beings, exists in the milieu of a social structure, and can be acquired by individuals and become part of their private realm. Suppose this distribution is entirely random.

In this world where every individual human being comes into existence as a product of the random combination of male and female genetic material, is subject to random variations in conditions and situations, and the wealth which accrues to each individual is acquired by a purely random process, how would wealth be distributed?

If a circle indicates an individual human being, W = wealth, and Rnd = the rule of random distribution of wealth, this social structure could be represented as in Figure 3.

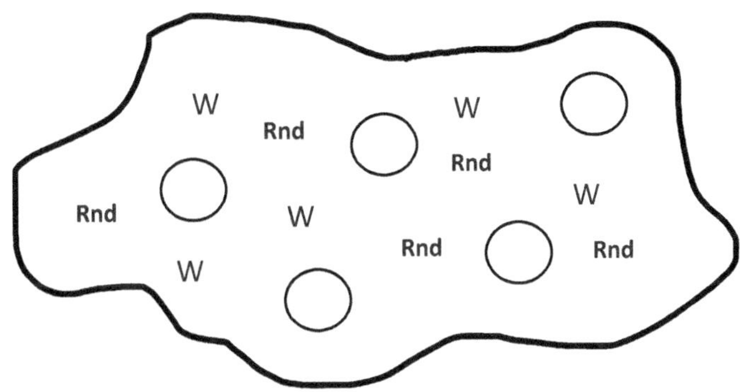

Figure 3: THE RULE OF THE RANDOM DISTRIBUTION OF WEALTH

Now suppose that, over the course of a year, there is a fixed sum of wealth to be distributed to all individuals.

Let's say there are 10,000 units of wealth to be distributed among 100 individuals over the course of a year and let's postulate that this distribution occurs in a completely random manner. How much wealth would be acquired by each individual?

If we plot on a horizontal axis the amount of wealth "units" acquired by each individual and on a vertical axis the number of individuals who had acquired a given amount of wealth over the course of a year, after which all the wealth is distributed, it will appear as a bell-shaped curve (Figure 4).

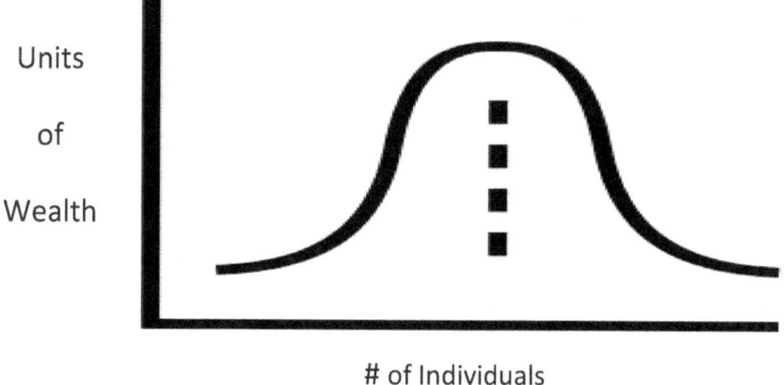

Figure 4: THE RANDOM DISTRIBTION OF WEALTH

Why?

The answer is provided by the laws of probability:

"If the observed measurement is the sum of many independent, small, random factors, the resulting measurements will take on values that are distributed in a pattern called the normal or gaussian distribution." (Primer of Biostatistics by Stanton A. Glantz, Ph.D. McGraw-Hill Book Company, Copyright 1981 by McGraw-Hill, Inc., pgs. 14-15).

If all the wealth of a nation which was created over the course of a year was randomly distributed, not every individual would enjoy equal wealth. A small number of individuals would be fortunate enough to acquire a large amount of wealth, a small number of individuals would have a small amount of wealth, and the majority would acquire an amount of wealth that was near the average between these two extremes.

Because such a distribution in this model is completely random, we cannot invoke the concepts of victims and oppressors. It is best to think about the differences between the "rich" and the "poor" in this situation as a function of pure luck. Although one could divide the population of individuals into the "haves" and "have nots," and even identify a group of individuals within such a population as "have a little and want more," these classifications are not due to the behavior of any one particular individual or a group of individuals. No one is at fault. There is no one to blame for the unequal distribution of wealth when the distribution is completely random.

5 THE LOTTERY

There are other ways to distribute wealth based purely on probability. Suppose 100 individuals each agree to put $100 into a pool. The pool would contain $10,000. Now suppose that each of these 100 people agree with each other to play this game: give all individuals a piece of paper and have them write their name on it. Fold each piece of paper up into a small square and throw these 100 pieces of paper into a bowl. Shake the bowl up. Pull out one piece of paper. The name of the individual on that one piece of paper gets all the money in the pool.

In this game, there will be one individual who, having put up $100, winds up in possession of $10,000. And all the other individuals in the pool will have taken a loss of $100 (Figure 5).

This distribution of wealth can be depicted graphically:

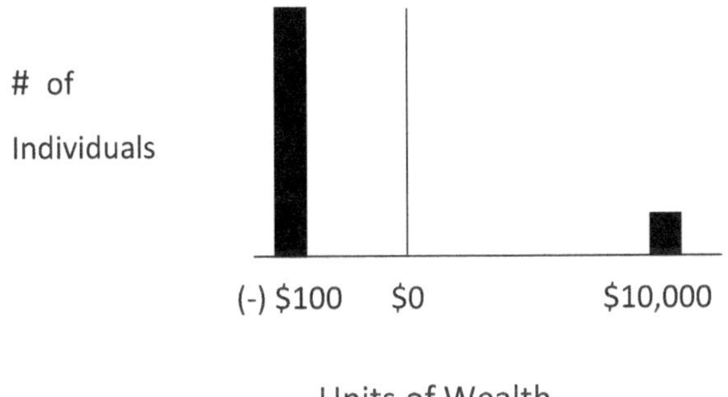

Figure 5: DISTRIBUTION OF WEALTH BY LOTTERY

In this situation, there are winners and losers. One wouldn't call the losers victims. And the winner, who might be considered rich, relatively speaking, would not be obligated to share the wealth so acquired with the losers.

Just as in the situation where there is a random distribution of wealth, one can identify in this lottery a "lucky" one and those who are unlucky, but one cannot say that anyone is at fault for the distribution of wealth that follows the completion of the lottery. There will be "the haves" and "the have nots" and perhaps even the "had a little, want more," but those who feel they "want more" is a function of the individual and how he feels and thinks about his situation rather than the mechanism and manner by which wealth is being distributed. If everyone agrees to play by certain rules, the consequences that accrue over time as a function of playing by those rules are intrinsic to the social situation itself. If one of the 99 individuals who did not win the lottery demands that the winner share his new-found wealth with the others, because it is only fair, he might be said to be a sore loser. And the individual who won the lottery and decides not to share his new-found wealth with others might be called out as "greedy." But such designations are what human beings bring to the situation. The designations are not intrinsic to the situation itself.

6 THE ORIGIN OF WEALTH

The social structure of human beings can be imagined as a situation in which individual human beings come into existence as random events, learn a set of rules and regulations which all are expected to follow, and live in a milieu of wealth and surrounded by a border that delineates this social structure. Each individual human being as a living unit is exposed over time to situations and opportunities (Figure 3A).

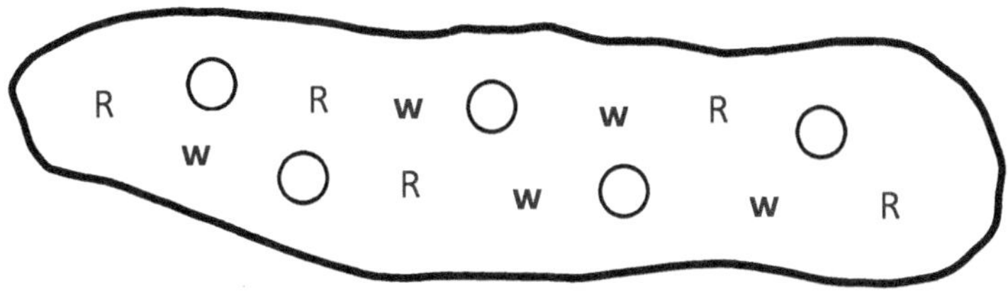

Figure 3A: HUMAN SOCIAL STRUCTURE WITH WEALTH

Within this social structure there exist units of wealth which have the attribute that they can be incorporated into the private realm of an individual.

How does such wealth come into being? What causes it to exist? How is it created? And how is the value of such wealth determined?

Suppose a human being has legitimate ownership of a tree that has grown into a mighty oak. Then this oak falls in the woods as a result of a powerful storm. He takes the wood and out of it fashions some beautiful wooden salad bowls. He takes the remaining pieces of wood and fashions them into neatly bundled packets of firewood. Call these creations "goods and services."

By chance, he comes upon a fellow human being who wants one of these creations. She wants a salad bowl. They make a deal. He gives her a salad bowl. In exchange she gives him a unit of value.

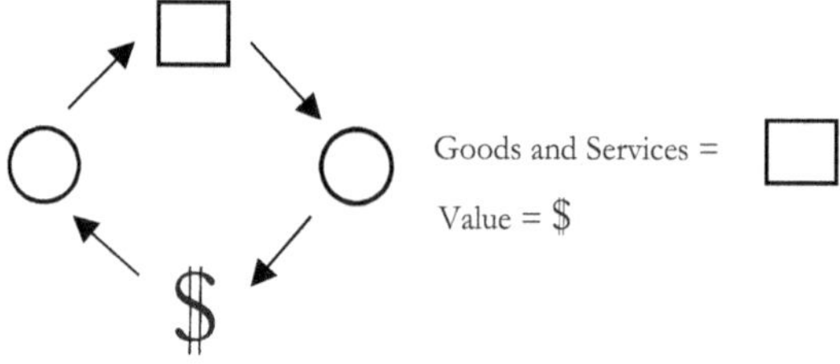

Figure 6: THE EXCHANGE OF GOODS AND SERVICES

This loop of activity is the primary act by which goods and services are exchanged between individuals living in a free society.

This is a voluntary exchange. There are no victims or oppressors. It is purely social cooperation where each human being participating in the exchange benefit.

For this exchange to occur, the woman must want the salad bowl more than the unit of value she is giving up. And he who created the salad bowl wants the unit of value she is willing to give him for it more than he wants the salad bowl itself.

We can portray the fact that both individuals are acting of their own free will by incorporating the expression, **E! FW** into the diagram. The "**E!**" is taken to mean "There exists" and "**FW**" stands for "Free Will."

Let's call the individual who is transferring the salad bowl to the other individual the "seller" and the individual who is accepting the salad bowl the "buyer."

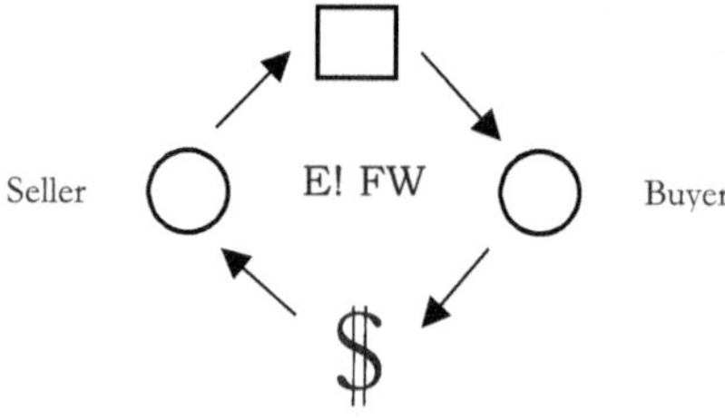

Figure 7: A WILLING BUYER TO A WILLING SELLER

This situation is often described as "a willing buyer to a willing seller." It is composed of the elements and relationships that are depicted in Figure 7.

The seller has created a form of wealth in creating goods and services. The value of that wealth can be thought of in terms of some standard unit, indicated by "$".

We can assume that most of the time the value, $, in this kind of exchange will be a positive number. Therefore, in most situations, $ > 0$.

Why?

The seller has used his time, energy, and ingenuity to create the salad bowl. He had to come up with the idea of making a salad bowl and then spent his time and energy actually fashioning it out of the wood of a fallen tree. He used up a limited resource, the wood of a fallen tree, to create the salad bowls. Altogether, this creates positive value.

7 THE FREE MARKET SYSTEM

In a social structure as depicted in Figure 7, there may be more than one buyer and there may be more than one seller. The fact that there may be more than one buyer or seller will impact the value, $, that becomes associated with the salad bowl.

Suppose another buyer comes along and offers the seller a value, $, for the salad bowl which is a greater amount than the original buyer offered. The price of the salad bowl may go up. Suppose someone else makes a salad bowl and offers it for a value, $, that is less than what the original seller agreed to when he allowed the first buyer to take possession of the salad bowl. The value of the salad bowl might go down.

The value of goods and services in a social situation with this kind of structure will be determined by this constellation of activity, which is the summation of all these individuals acting of their own free will.

An extended order of human cooperation can be envisioned as emerging where an innumerable number of individuals producing all kinds of goods and services enter into all kinds of inter-related exchanges. (Figure 8).

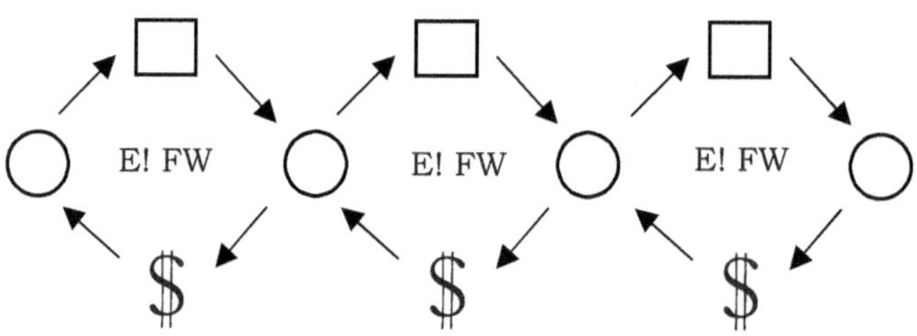

Figure 8: THE FREE MARKET SYSTEM

8 CHARITY AND THEFT

In the exchange of goods and services between two human beings, concepts of a moral nature inevitably arise.

For instance, suppose the buyer is unable to give the seller a positive value, $, for the salad bowl but indicates she would like to take possession of it anyway. The man who made the salad bowl decides to give the salad bowl to her anyway. Its value in this particular transaction therefore is zero. $ = 0. Thus it becomes a gift. This could also be seen as charity. It is the transfer of a good or service with nothing expected in return.

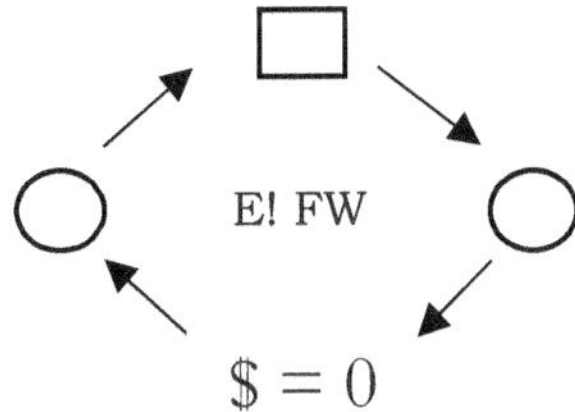

Figure 9: CHARITY

What would we call this situation if we took free will out of the exchange, but kept the value, $, equal to 0? Suppose the woman took the salad bowl from the man, against his will, and gave him nothing in return. That would be called theft.

Let ØE! = There does not exist.

Let ØE! FW = There does not exist free will.

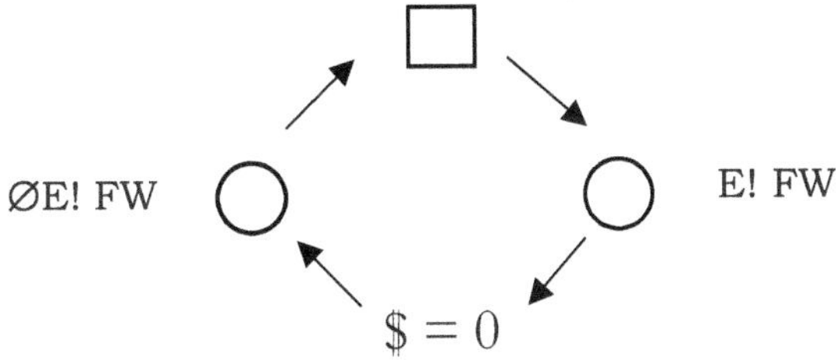

Figure 10: THEFT

Charity and theft have almost identical forms. They are composed of the same elements in the same relationships except for the fact that free will has been removed from one side of the exchange. The woman is acting of her own free will, but in the second situation, almost identical in form, the man is not. His salad bowl is being taken away from him against his will and he gets nothing of value in return.

The difference between charity and theft, then, is whether or not the exchange of goods and services for a value equal to zero is occurring in the context of free will for all individuals involved in the exchange.

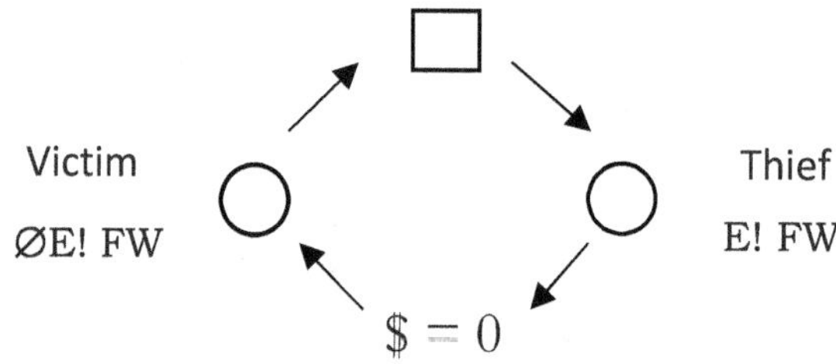

Figure 10A: THEFT

9 WHAT IS A FACT?

Thus far we have introduced concepts of the individual, wealth, the distribution of wealth, free will, charity, theft, and ideas about the social structure of human beings.

Are these ideas facts or opinions?

What is a fact?

A **fact** exists when the idea about something which is held in the mind **fits the form** of that same thing as it exists in reality. We all know from experience what an idea is. But what do we mean when we speak of the form of an idea? **Form is an arrangement of elements and the relationships between them**.

The form of a "day," for instance, consists of time, generally thought of in units of hours, composed of 24 such units, and can be thought of both as a linear pattern, that progresses indefinitely into the future (i.e. "day after day"), and as a cycle that repeats the same pattern again and again, each time the earth rotates about its axis (e.g. an analogue wall clock).

Let's apply this assertion of what a fact is to the concept of theft which has been introduced here. The elements operative in the idea of theft include the concept of the individual, private property, and free will. It is the relationships between these elements that allow one to understand the form of theft. Since the idea of theft involves the transfer of private property of some sort, from one individual human being to another, the idea requires the existence of at least two distinct individuals. It also requires the concept of private property. If all goods, once created, were owned by all the human beings in a society, there would be no such thing as theft, because one cannot steal something that is already owned. Theft also involves the concept of free will as well as the exact opposite: the absence of free will. If both individuals are acting of their own free will in the exchange, the concept of theft doesn't apply.

So, if one human being accuses another of theft, to prove that to be a fact we would have to prove the existence of these specific kinds of elements and relationships and also prove that the actions that constituted the theft occurred in a social context defined by certain rules and regulations that the individuals involved in the act of theft both agreed to abide by.

The thief could argue in his defense that he does not believe in the idea of private property. In a society where all individual human beings accept as a given the concept of private property, and such a concept is protected by the law, theft becomes an illegal act; and a civil society is maintained by upholding the law protecting private property. But in an ill-defined social situation where the concept of private property is taken as arbitrary and debatable, the very idea of theft becomes arbitrary and debatable.

One can envision the chaos that would ensue if the basic concepts inherent to the existence of a civil society became unstable and subject to change by an arbitrary or capricious process that is not agreed to or accepted by the citizens of that civil society. It would create a malignant social environment. The social organism we call civil society would be subject to instability and possibly eventual death.

Most individuals living in the United States of America would agree with the **proposition** that there exists something called theft. But to actually establish that such a proposition, which is to say **the expression of various elements and their relationships to each other**, is true and is therefore a fact, we would have to demonstrate that all those individuals living in the USA agree to or are otherwise obligated to accept a host of other concepts that constitute and are at play in the idea of theft.

A fact is a proposition that mirrors reality by way of analogy. More often than not, a proposition which we take to be true and therefore expresses a fact will contain other ideas that also have to be established as facts. And, when we do this, sometimes we find ourselves coming across ideas which cannot be proven as fact by the scientific method of hypothesis generation and experimentation. Instead, they are ideas which we take as true only because of mutual agreement and not true in the sense that the idea can be proven to be true using science. In the realm of the structure of human society, many facts about it are ultimately constructed with or derived from arbitrary notions such as whether to assume there exists the free will of the individual, private property, and whether or not we decide to take the individual or the group as the primary unity of activity in human society.

The most successful human societies have evolved as a process of natural selection where the ideas and concepts about the structure of human society that are operational have been selected to be utilized by human beings because those particular ideas and concepts, when put into play, have created the most successful extended order of human cooperation and allow the most robust creation of wealth and diversity of ideas for all individual human beings in that society to share.

It is a fact that, in the United States of the America, "There exists theft." It is a fact that, in the USA, "There exists charity." But these propositions express facts because in the USA the concept of private property and the free will of the individual are taken as inalienable rights and protected by law.

10 SLAVERY

What is the form of slavery? We have already established that the form of theft can be expressed as in Figure 10 and charity has an almost identical form, as expressed in Figure 9. The only difference between the two is whether or not there exists free will for all individuals involved in the exchange.

How can we express the form of slavery?

The feeling and thought of something being private is part of the human condition and is established in infancy. A human being's body is his or her own. Thoughts can be private. Feelings can be private. If a human being uses his time and energy to create something, and not a single other human being contributes to that creation, the creation is, in its inception, private. If the human being transfers that creation of his or her own free will to another human being in exchange for something else of value which is agreed to and acceptable for all parties involved, that thing of value becomes, likewise, something private in the realm of an individual who did not originally create it. It is owned by another individual human being who is someone other than its creator. And thus the concept of ownership is born.

In this sense, we can represent each individual existing within a boundary or border. Anything within the border is private property. Anything outside the border is not private property.

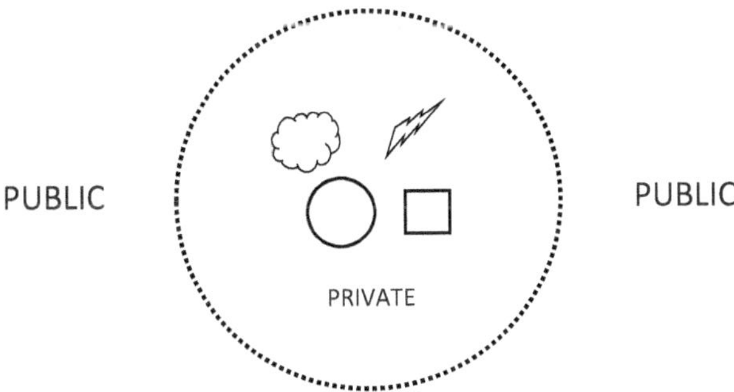

Figure 11: PRIVATE PROPERTY: Items within the circle are *private property*.

Feelings, ideas, and material goods are all things that can exist in the private realm, as private property.

A human being can own all kinds of things. Food. Cars. Houses. Books. Even living things, like plants. And dogs and cats.

But a fundamental tenant of civil human society is that a human being cannot own another human being. Each human being exists as an individual human being and cannot be owned by another human being.

The form of slavery would be depicted as:

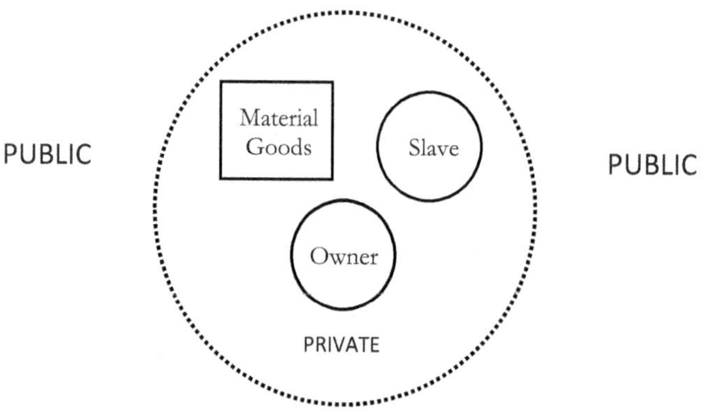

Figure 12: SLAVERY

In civil human society, slavery is prohibited. It is not allowed. It is against the rules.

Where there exists the individual human being, there exists the concept of privacy. Where there exist physical things that are part of an individual's realm, there exists a universe of private things. Where there is no conception of the human being as an individual, there is nothing that is private.

The meaning of slavery is that one human being owns another human being. In a society grounded in the concept that all human beings are created equal, this is forbidden. If one human being owns another human being, the two human beings are not equal.

As physical specimens each individual is unique and no individual is exactly the same as another individual human being. But, in a society where there is a rule that no human being is allowed to exist as an object in the private realm of another human being, in this context, human beings can be thought of as equals.

11 SOCIAL STRUCTURE

A **structure** is something that is **composed of various objects.** A house can be built with wood or bricks and includes things like windows and doors. A face generally includes eyes, a nose, and a mouth. Music is composed of sound and silence in time. The objects that compose a structure can be real or imaginary. A wall demarcating a property line can be made of stone or plastic fence posts, but the property line itself is ultimately an imaginary construct on the Earth's surface.

Human society is likewise a structure that is composed of various objects. Human beings are one of them. In fact, the human being is the fundamental object without which human society would not exist:

OBJECT 1: An Individual human being

It follows directly that an individual human being's body as well as the thoughts and feelings of that human being are also essential objects that compose human society:

OBJECT 2: Human thought   OBJECT 3: Human feeling

The body and mind of a human being each belong to that individual human being and to no one else.

We can represent the body and mind of a human being by a circle the circumference of which is a solid line:

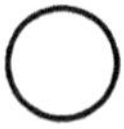

OBJECT 4: A token of an individual human being

We can take this circle to indicate the existence of a human being. All human beings exist in the realm of time.

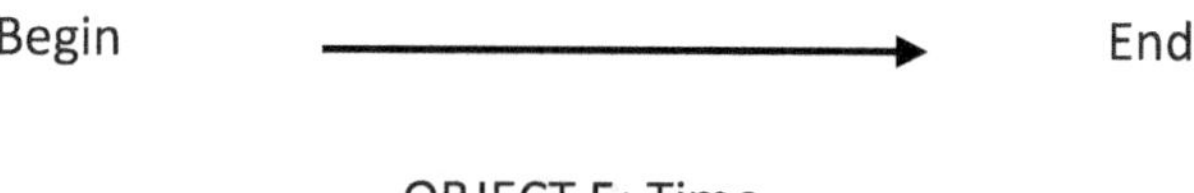

OBJECT 5: Time

A human being's mind and body and his or her thoughts and feelings can be considered "private." And so we create a distinction between private and not private:

OBJECT 6: The distinction between private and public

This distinction between "private" and "not private" need not be drawn as a straight vertical line. We could just as well draw it as a circle and put the things that are "private" within the circle. And everything outside the circle can be considered "not private" or "public."

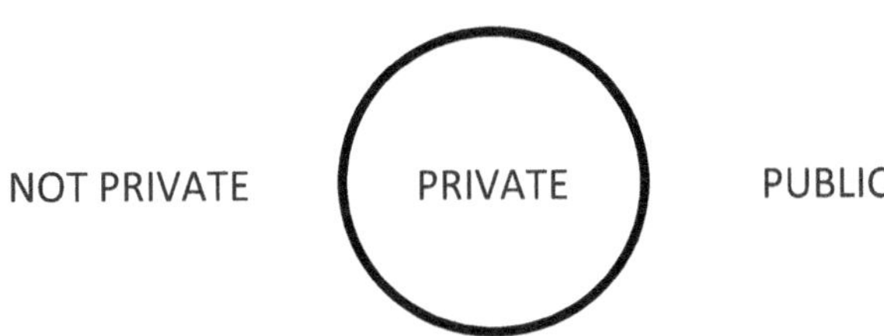

We could draw the circumference of the circle as a line constructed with dashes, to indicate that objects can cross between the public and private realm.

OBJECT 7: Private and public spaces

Each individual human being can express his or her thoughts and feelings.

OBJECT 8: Expression of thought or feeling

The expression of the thoughts and feelings of an individual human being can and do under certain circumstances become public.

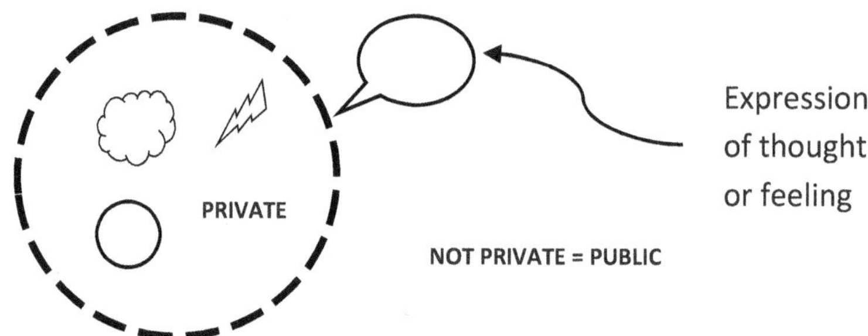

Figure 13: THE PUBLIC EXPRESSION OF THOUGHT AND FEELING

Individual human beings can and do make objects of value or provide services of valve.

Figure 14: THE CREATION OF GOODS AND SERVICES

These goods and services may be private when first created and then, under certain circumstances, become public.

Figure 15: TRANSFER OF GOODS AND SERVICES FROM PRIVATE TO PUBLIC REALM

In order for human beings to exchange goods and services amongst themselves, they may create objects that indicate the existence of valve:

OBJECT 10: Value

Human beings can then create a relationship between goods and services and objects of value.

Figure 16: RELATIONSHIP BETWEEN GOODS AND SERVICES AND VALUE

The social structure of human beings is composed of various objects:

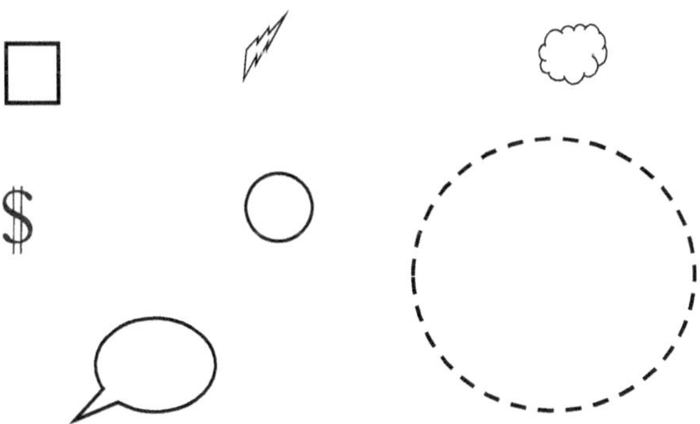

And the activity of human beings within this sea of objects is guided by various rules and relationships which guide the interaction between these social objects. These rules and relationships are objects too that compose the social structure of human beings.

$$R = \text{RULES AND RELATIONSHIPS}$$

OBJECT 12: Rules and Relationships

Rules and relationships are one of the most important objects that exist within the structure of human society.

There is another object that comes into existence with the creation of human social structures. The social structure of human beings can be distinguished from a collection of human beings who exist with no structure.

The distinction between a human social structure and a collection of human beings without a structure need not be drawn as a straight vertical line. We could just as well draw it as a boundary and put the objects which define the structure within the boundary and human beings who exist without a structure outside the boundary.

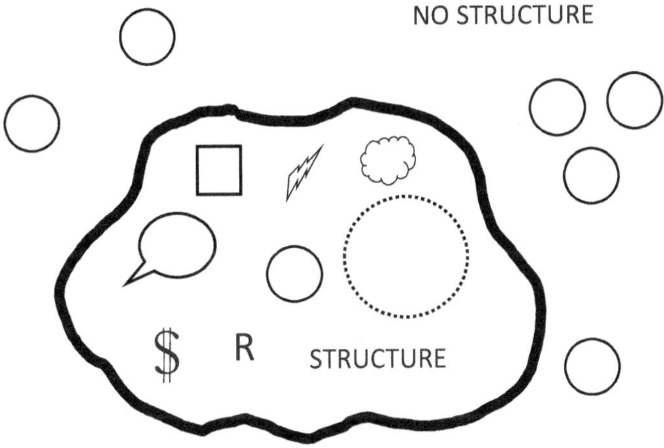

Figure 17: HUMAN SOCIAL STRUCTURE

The bold line indicating this distinction can be conceived of as a border that distinguishes a structured human society from a structureless human society.

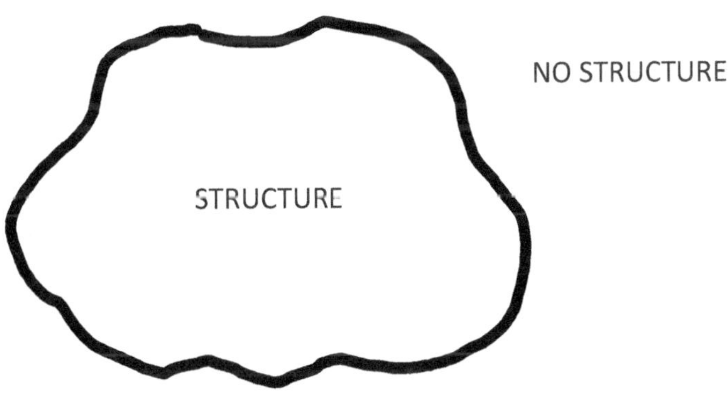

OBJECT 13: Border

Different human social structures can come into existence simply by changing some of the objects within the social structure. For instances, there might exist one human social structure that contains no rules. This kind of social structure could then be distinguished from a human social structure with rules. Or a human social system might not allow for the existence of private property. Individual human beings existing in these different types of human social structures would have different experiences.

Figure 18: DIFFERENT HUMAN SOCIAL STRUCTURES

The lives which human beings experience are a function of the objects that exist in the social structure in which they live. Borders are used not only to distinguish a human social structure from a non-structured human social situation, but also to distinguish one human social structure from another.

12 RULES OF ENGAGEMENT

The abstract notions that define the structure of human societies, such as thoughts, feelings, goods and services, value, rules, and distinctions between public and private domains, can be applied to a variety of human social structures.

Anyone who has driven a car or other form of motor vehicle understands how these objects that compose the social structures of human beings become operationalized.

In the case of the social structure of human beings who drive motor vehicles, one understands that a human being may own a car that he or she keeps in the private domain of his or her garage or driveway, but on occasion might have opportunity to take that motor vehicle out on public land and drive it on roads built for this purpose:

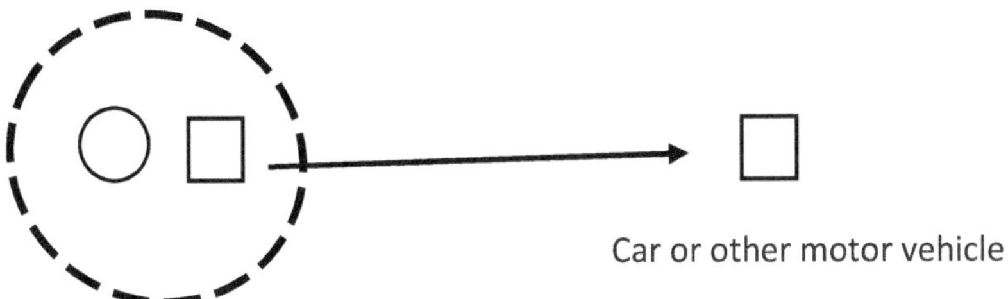

In order to do so, all individuals who drive motor vehicles on public roads are required to learn and master the "rules of the road" and apply these rules in the operation of the motor vehicle. In fact, they must get a license that is testimony to the fact that the driver understands and promises to obey the rules of the road.

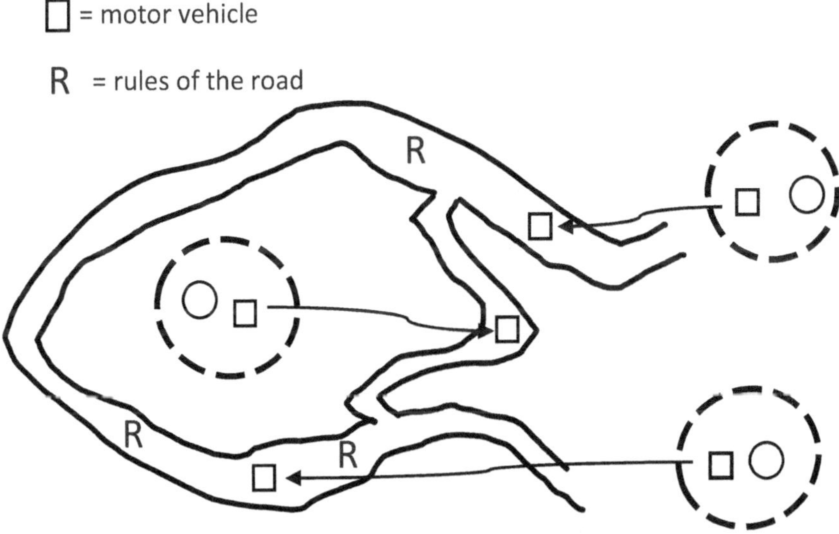

Figure 19: RULES OF THE ROAD FOR DRIVERS OF MOTOR VEHICLES

One can only imagine the chaos that would ensue in a social structure that allowed the activity of motorized vehicles of transportation to operate on public roads without a shared system of rules of the road.

These rules of the road can and do vary and distinguish one such social structure from another. For instance, in some countries all motor vehicles must drive on the right side of the road. In others, they must drive on the left side of the road.

R_R = motor vehicles must drive on right side of road

R_L = motor vehicles must drive on left side of road

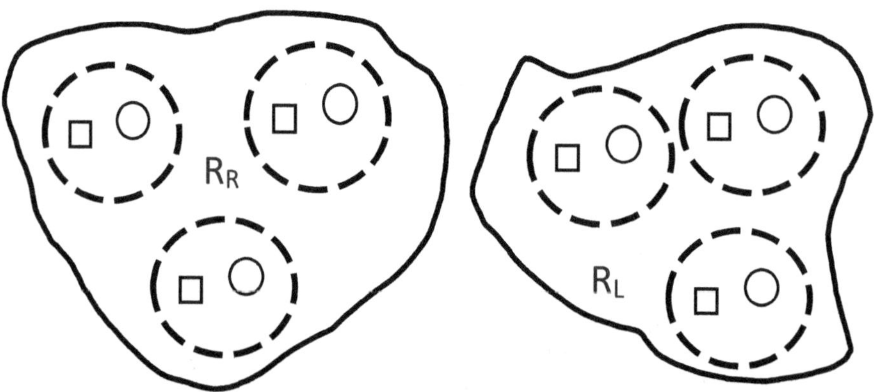

Figure 20: DIFFERENT RULES OF THE ROAD CREATE DISTINCT SOCIAL STRUCTURES

These two social structures are identical except for the fact that the rules pertaining to the operation of motor vehicles are different. This not only makes the two social structures distinct; it makes them incompatible. It is not that one rule, R_R, is better or correct and the other, R_L, is worse or wrong. It is just that either all cars drive on the right side of the road or all cars drive on the left. You cannot have a social structure for motor vehicles where some drivers drive on the right of the road and others drive on the left without increasing the probability of accidents.

Thus, the rules by which human beings and other objects that compose the social structure are related are essential in defining the structure of that social system.

Here are eight rules or concepts by which some human social systems might operate:

Thou shall not kill
Thou shall not steal
Thou shall not lie.
There shall not exist slaves. (ØE! Slaves)
There shall exist individual free will. (E! FW)
There shall exist private property.
Thou shall obey the rules.
A willing buyer to a willing seller.

A set of rules such as this is composed of concepts that indicate relationships between human beings that ultimately are arbitrary. That is, one could just as well construct a society where the rule is that it is okay to kill other human beings, or to steal, or to lie. One could have a society where it is acceptable to have slaves, or in which the free will of the individual human being is not allowed. But such a social structure would shape for each individual human being a very different kind of life and human experience.

The point is, the rules that human beings choose to live by, arbitrary or not, are an essential object in defining their social structure. Change the rules, and the fundamental nature of the social structure changes, even if all the other objects in the social system remain the same.

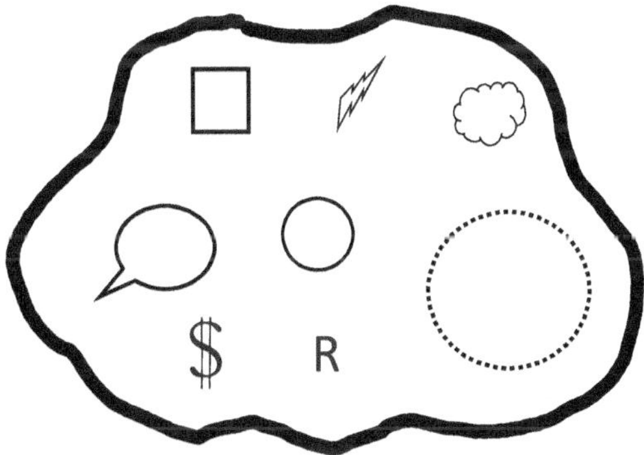

Figure 17: HUMAN SOCIAL STRUCTURE

Most human social structures have not just one rule, but a set of rules; many might have several sets of rules with a hierarchy defined among those different sets of rules.

If a set of rules consists of a total number of "X" rules, it can be represented as a sum of all these rules:

$$\sum_{N=1}^{X} R$$

OBJECT 14: Set of Rules

And the hierarchy of rules might be represented as:

$$\sum_{N=1}^{X} R1 \quad > \quad \sum_{N=1}^{X} R2 \quad > \quad \sum_{N=1}^{X} R3$$

Figure 21: HIERARCHY OF SETS OF RULES

13 THE SHAPING FORCES OF EVIL

Thought experiment: a human being goes around cutting off the hands of other human beings as they sleep. His motivations are unclear. But he keeps doing it.

He cuts off the hands of little babies. He cuts off the hands of school children. He cuts off the hands of adults.

He does not have permission to do so. He just does it.

Is this individual Evil?

Many would say yes.

Why would a human being consider this action Evil?

If a human being exists within a social structure where there exists free will, could not the argument be made that this individual is exercising his free will?

Some might argue that the situation is not that simple. There are two individual human beings involved in this situation and the one who is cutting off the hands of other individuals is violating an equally important concept: private property.

The hands of a human being are part of his or her body and one's body is not the property of any other human being. Therefore, one human being has no right to cut off the hands of another human being.

Human social structure is composed of a number of objects which are intrinsic to the social condition. To disregard or disrupt those objects, to alter the fundamental nature of its elements and violate the relationships between them, is to undermine human society itself.

Evil has its origin in those acts that undermine, violate, or ultimately destroy those objects that are intrinsic to the social structure which a group of human beings have chosen to and agree to live by. This in turn tears apart the fabric of that social structure, destroying the human activity and interaction that once existed and replacing the social objects, its elements and the rules and regulations which dictate or guide their relationships, by a process that violates or destroys these social objects.

Human society has a structure, consisting of a border or boundary within which are other social objects, including individual human beings, thoughts, feelings, goods and services, value, and relationships. From these elements and relationships still more social objects might be derived, such as private property and free will. The relationships and rules that exist between the various elements of human society create conditions and loops of inter-related activity analogous to a living organism, such as a living cell, which is the smallest unit of objects found in Nature which forms a living system.

The shaping forces of Evil have their roots in those things that function to destroy the objects of which human society is composed, including its elements or the rules and relationships between those elements, both of which are essential to the operation of the social structure of human beings.

Evil is rooted in acts that destroy the objects of civil society: acts that destroy human beings, destroy thoughts and feelings, destroy the notion of the private realm of the individual, destroy goods and services, destroy the notion of value, destroy rules and relationships, or destroy the boundaries which demarcate, maintain, and protect the interaction of these objects in their social milieu.

In this regard it is worthwhile to note that, **without altering or changing any of the fundamental elements** of human society, such as the human beings who compose it, the living organism represented by a **human social structure can be altered and potentially destroyed simply by changing the rules and relationships** which characterize the mutual interactions between its fundamental elements.

Therein lies a kernel of Evil.

14 REALITY, PERCEPTION, AND CONCEPTION

There is a lot of talk these days about science and admonishment to "follow the science." What is science?

Most understand that science is used to inform us about reality. Somehow, science speaks to reality. And science is seen as something different than fiction and even science fiction.

But what is science and how does it work? And is there a science that is applicable to the social structures of human beings?

Human beings are born as unique individuals and exist in a matrix wherein each individual interacts with other human beings. This social structure gives rise to distinct units which can take on many forms. Family. Friends. School. Villages, towns, and cities. States. Countries. All these different social structures share certain identifiable features.

Most would agree that, when we look at the social structure of human beings, anywhere that it exists, it can look something like this:

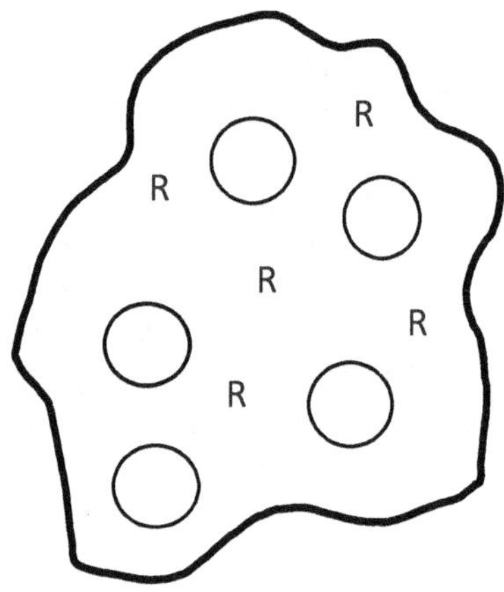

Figure 22: A GENERAL CONCEPT OF HUMAN SOCIAL STRUCTURE

The image in Figure 22 is an idea. It is not reality itself and, although it is perceived through the eyes, it is not a perception of reality itself. It is an image of the reality of the social structure of human society. It is a concept.

There are relationships between perception, conception, and reality. And the relationships between perception, conception, and reality can and do differ between individuals.

Scientific thought seeks a state where the logical form of conception is wholly analogous to the logical form of reality and the logical form of reality is derived from and is wholly analogous to the logical form of human perception.

Reality doesn't differ between individuals. It acts and behaves in a manner independent of the individual, although individuals can and do interact with reality itself in different ways. But the perception and conception of reality can and does differ among individuals.

When a baby is born, the perceptions which are experienced by the infant exist as an amorphous blur. The baby hears things and sees things. The baby feels its body being touched and it touches things. The baby tastes things and smells things. All these sensed and felt things exist as utterly formless at first.

Gradually the infant begins to distinguish in this formless universe of perceptions distinct objects. Those objects may be other individual human beings. Or food. Or even something as abstract as time. Many of these objects become elements in the infant's universe of experience. Other objects become relations between elements.

When everything gets dark and quiet, it is time to sleep. When things around me get light and noisier, I awake. Sometimes I am awake when things are dark and quiet. Sometimes I am asleep when it is light and noisy.

Before the infant has any command of language, its universe of perceptions takes on a form consisting of various elements and their relationships.

And this is the basis of the infant's ideas or concepts about the world.

Very early on, the infant experiences three classes of ideas. One class of ideas can be described as true. This is a class of ideas in which the elements and relationships which make up a particular idea are wholly congruent to the infant's perceptions and also to the reality which gives rise to those perceptions. There is another class of ideas which are exactly the opposite: the elements and relationships which make up a particular idea are not congruent to the infant's perceptions or to the reality which gives rise to those perceptions. This class of ideas is called false. And then there is a class of ideas which lie somewhere in between true and false, either because the ideas seem to be partially true, or partially false, or it is just not known whether the ideas are true or false.

As the infant grows and develops, there is a dynamic relationship between reality, perception, and conception.

In this way an individual's conception of truth is continually evolving, as are his or her ideas about what is false and what ideas have an unknown truth value.

Is the simple distinction between truth and falsehood in and of itself scientific thinking? Not really.

If a child goes to a zoo and sees a zebra, the conceptual process might be something like this:

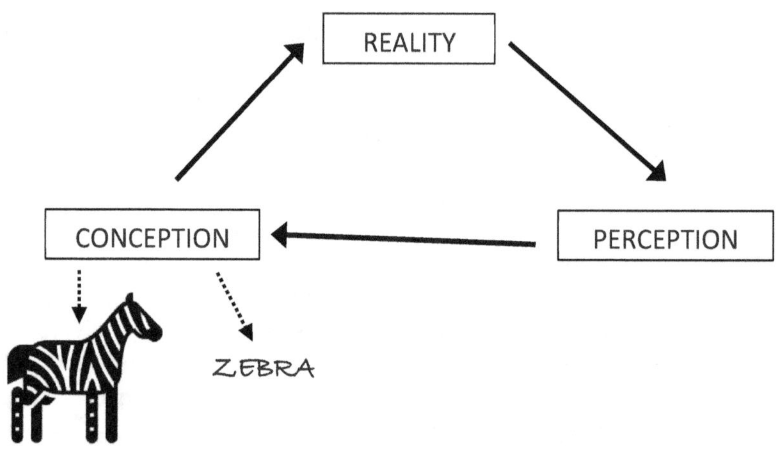

Figure 23: RELATIONSHIPS BETWEEN REALITY, PERCEPTION, AND CONCEPTION

And in the bird house, the child might see an owl:

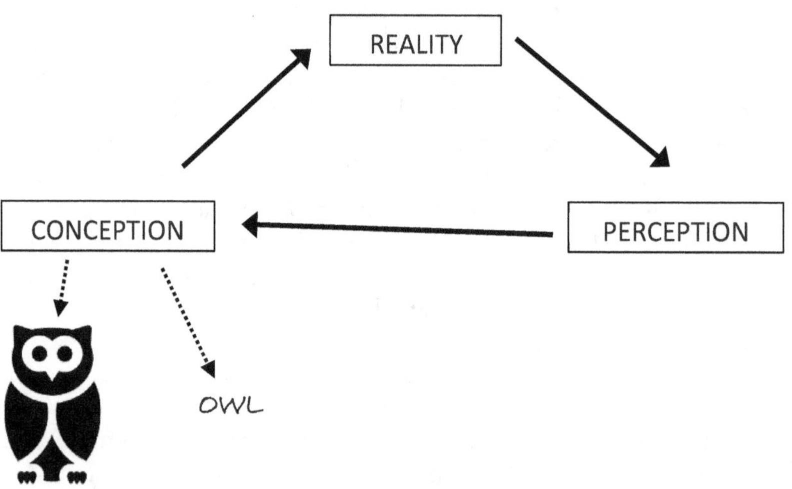

These relationships are true, but one would not consider them scientific.

Science takes a deep dive into reality to come up with ideas that far exceed simple perception and classification.

One hot summer day, that same child who went to the zoo is given a glass of cold water with some ice in it by an older sibling. The child takes a drink and then goes on playing with his toys.

When the child returns for some more water, the ice is gone. The glass contains only water and no ice.

"What happened to the ice?" asks the child.

"It melted," responds an older sibling.

And the older sibling explains to the child that all matter is composed of atoms, tiny objects that a human being cannot see with the naked eye. And these atoms can bond together to form groups of atoms called molecules.

The sibling goes on: "Water is made up of molecules composed of two hydrogen atoms and one oxygen atom. And the water molecules themselves come together in groups with bonds between them. The nature of the bonds between water molecules changes when the temperature changes. In liquid water, the bonds are flexible. But if we put water in a place that is really cold, like the freezer, the bonds get more rigid. And when that happens, water becomes ice."

And then the sibling suggests they do an experiment. They take the child's glass of water and put it in the freezer.

"We'll come back tonight. And you'll see. That water will be ice."

Later that night, the child goes back to the freezer and fetches his glass. And the older sibling was right. His glass of water is now a glass of ice.

And at that very moment, the child understood the meaning of water in a very different way than he had ever before. Until then, the word water triggered in his mind an object just like the words zebra and owl and had a relationship to other objects in his experience. He knew water as something he could drink. Or bathe in. Or swim in. He knew water as rain or something that came out of the sprinkler to water the lawn. These were all relationships he had to water.

He had not known that ice was water. And that ice and water were different forms of the same thing – each composed of identical molecules.

But now he understood water to be made up of objects called molecules that had their own external relationships between themselves. And when those external relationships changed, so did the nature of water itself.

He now understood that the form and substance of water changed materially not by changing the elements of which it was composed, those molecules that, as individual objects, he could not see or touch, but by changing only the relationships between those elements.

This change in his ideas about water forever changed the way he saw the world around him.

It was easy to see objects when they were elements, like water, zebras, and owls. But objects that exist as relationships, if one could call them objects at all, were not visible. They were things that existed in between material objects and had an effect on their form and substance and how they behaved. And those relationships had a profound impact on the nature of reality.

The next day a friend was over and the child told his friend what he had learned about water.

The friend replied: "Hey, if warming ice makes water, maybe if we heat water up, we can get even more water."

Together the child and his friend then set about to heat up some water. They took a pot and filled it with water. They put the pot on the stove and turned the heat up under the pot. Soon bubbles began forming in the water.

They stared. Wow! Something is happening. They kept watching. Soon white vapor began rising from the water. But instead of more water being made, the level of the water in the pot began to go down. And eventually the water disappeared.

The kids looked at each other. They stared in disbelief.

And the child went to his older sibling and asked, "What happened?"

"You broke apart the bonds between the water molecules," he replied.

"When you change the relationships between elements, you change the structure of the thing. And sometimes, by changing the relationships between the elements, you destroy the thing itself. And it disappears."

"You didn't destroy the water molecules. But you destroyed the form of water that you valued the most."

15 MS. KEYER

Ms. Keyer was a young, vibrant individual. And to all, she seemed to have a heart of gold.

And all year she taught her first graders that $1 + 1 = 3$.

Sunset Lower School was large enough to have two first-grade sections. One was called *Class Lavender* and the other was called *Class Rose*. Years ago they were named class A and class B, but some parents and teachers objected, arguing that class A might be assumed to be better than class B. For similar reasons the names class 1 and class 2 would not do, so they all decided to throw neutral letters of the alphabet into a hat and a randomly selected student randomly pulled the letters L and R from the hat. Each letter was then randomly assigned to a first-grade class by a randomly selected teacher and then ratified at a school meeting, which included the entire school community. Then a class name was chosen, using the assigned letter as the first letter in the chosen name.

Mr. Cromugedun was the teacher of the Rose Class. He was a partially bald, white-haired, and older individual, energetic, spirited, and with crystal-clear eyes.

And all year he taught his first-graders that 1 + 1= 2.

As luck would have it, Ms. Keyer had 41 children in her class. Mr. Cromugedun had 37.

On the first day of second grade, all the second-graders in a combined class assembly took a vote.

"What is 1 + 1?"

Forty former first-graders voted "3." And 38 voted "2." It turned out that the 40 former first-graders who voted "3" as the answer to the question "What is 1 + 1?" were all from Ms. Keyer's class.

"The wisdom of the minority." quipped Mr. Cromugedun.

But there were 41 students in Ms. Keyer's class and only 40 of them voted that "3" was the answer to the question, "What is 1 + 1?"

It turned out that one of Ms. Keyer's students, Jacob Singleton, got the answer to this question on Ms. Keyer's final exam wrong. He had answered 1 + 1 = 2.

Ms. Keyer had corrected Jacob's test, and she told him that 1 + 1 was 3, but he stuck to his guns.

All during his year in first grade, Jacob had been experimenting. He had taken two of his favorite balls and put them together on a shelf in his room. And he could see that one ball put together with another ball turned out to be two balls. And this happened whenever he took one object and put another one just like it together. It always turned out that he found himself with two of such objects. Two cookies. Two pencils. Two toy trucks. The result of putting one object together with another object just like it was to have two of those objects, not three.

Mr. Cromugedun remarked to Jacob's Mom later that day: "Jacob will grow up to be a noble young soul."

"Jacob has the gumption to figure out what is right and sticks to his guns. Even in the face of opposition by most of the others," Mr. Cromugedun continued. "He's going to be - actually, he is already - a noble young soul."

16 KIDS IN THE WHITE HOUSE

Intelligent and highly educated individuals can make conceptual mistakes, particularly when the concepts they create are derived from misinformation, disinformation, or lack of information.

Empathetic people can misdirect their empathy, particularly when they fail to fully appreciate the nature of Evil and choose instead to see the world through a prism of ultimate and pure goodness.

Ignorance can be extraordinarily dangerous, particularly to highly educated individuals, who tend to underestimate their own, and live under the assumption that his or her knowledge is so extensive and all-encompassing that that there is little more that needs to be learned or understood to extend the worldview presently possessed.

Peril exists when we seek to change things but do not fully appreciate the complex relations that hold those things together. In such situations, we might fail to define problems appropriately and then come up solutions that not only do not work but in fact make things worse than they were before there was even an attempt to solve the perceived problem.

When well-intentioned human beings, indeed highly educated individuals in positions of great power, seek to make the world a better place by manipulating the objects of human social reality, without the benefit of an adequate or sufficient conception of the reality of those human social systems, catastrophe may well linger just around the corner, a decade or two away, or perhaps within the reach of one or two generations. Such individuals can be called by the name "intellistupidons" and, when left to their own devices, create "intellistupidoms," kingdoms built upon illogical or unrealistic conceptions by self-identified intelligent individuals.

The fact that the story of Ms. Keyer in Chapter 15 may seem humorous should not detract from the fact that our subject matter here is deadly serious.

Can you imagine if there ever came a day when the collective knowledge of men and women was at once and completely wiped out? No knowledge of how to build airplanes, or cars or bikes, no knowledge of how to make movies, or print books, magazines, and newspapers, no knowledge of how to make computers, or cell phones, or televisions, no knowledge of how to build houses, chairs, and tables, no knowledge of cloth and clothes, no knowledge of pumps and engines, heaters, air conditions, stoves, and washing machines. No knowledge of farming or irrigation. No knowledge of physics, chemistry, or biology. No knowledge at all.

But have we in like manner lost our knowledge of social liberty, freedom, and private property? Do we not know the meaning of slavery and theft? Do we not understand the purpose and usefulness of competition - even though this knowledge has been articulated and to a large extent worked out over the generations of humankind that has preceded the current generation of human beings? Is the meaning of individual liberty disappearing from the collective mind called the United States of America?

In the grand transition from organized religion to atheism and a secular society, have we lost our understanding of morality?

Are we all just kids now, devoid of precious knowledge and understanding?

Worse yet, are the ideas that came before now scorned as conservative, traditional, and equated with the archaic? Are we left only with a future of ideas to be worked out and developed, and endless progress whose yet unproven value resides only in the fact that it is new? Or worse, not new but in fact old, tried, been there and done that, and only new through the eyes of ignorance?

LIST OF FIGURES

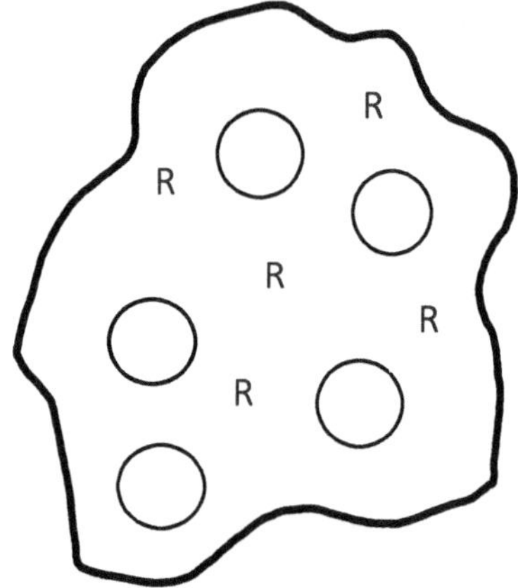

Figure 1: HUMAN SOCIAL STRUCTURE

Figure 2: THE INDIVIDAL HUMAN BEING

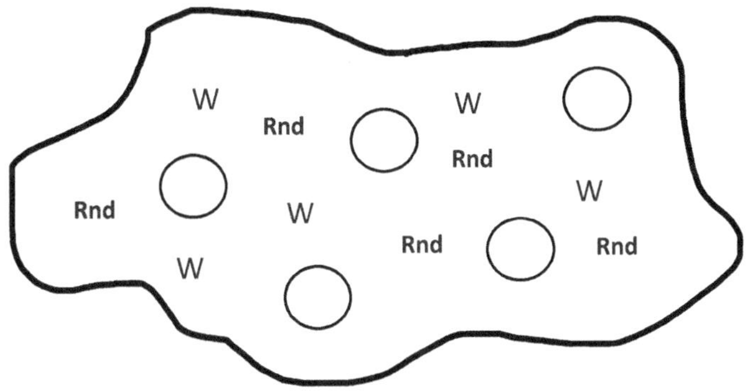

Figure 3: THE RULE OF THE RANDOM DISTRIBUTION OF WEALTH

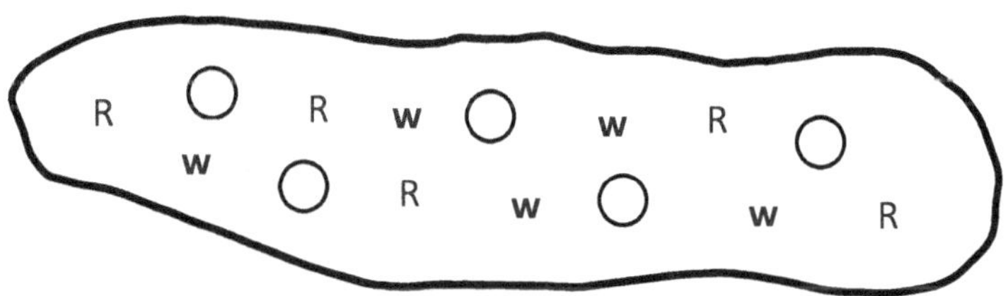

Figure 3A: HUMAN SOCIAL STRUCTURE WITH WEALTH

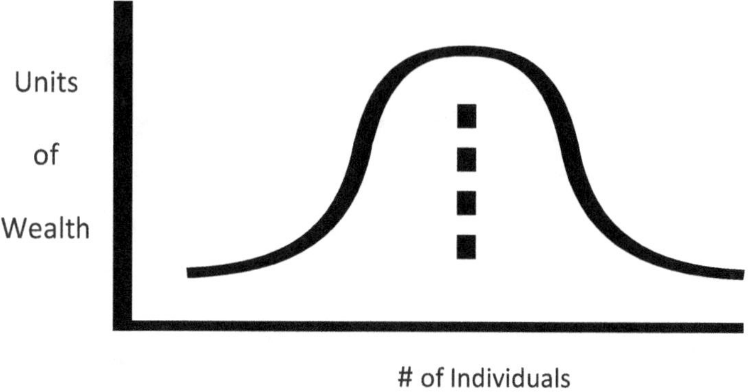

Figure 4: THE RANDOM DISTRIBTION OF WEALTH

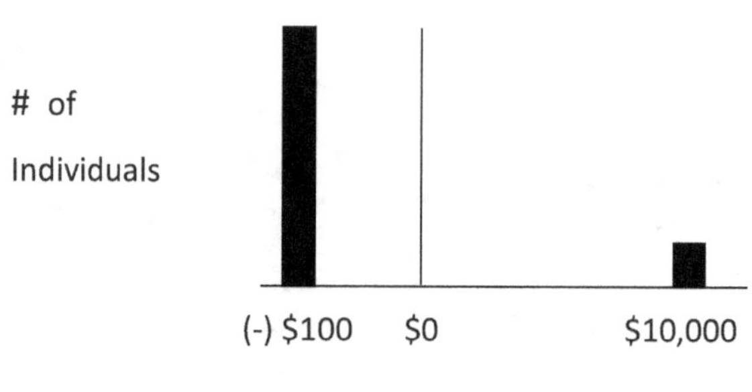

Figure 5: DISTRIBUTION OF WEALTH BY LOTTERY

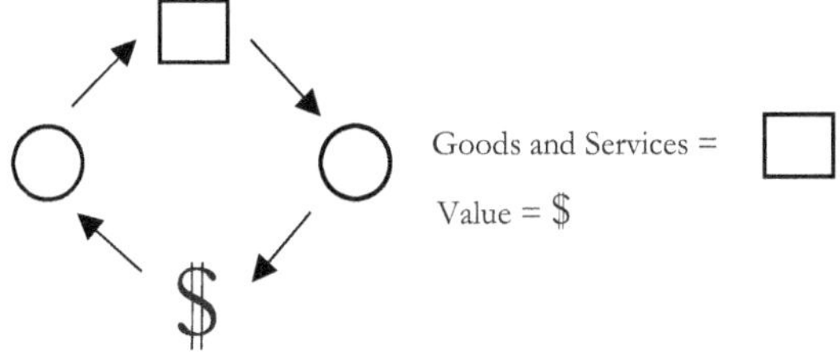

Figure 6: THE EXCHANGE OF GOODS AND SERVICES

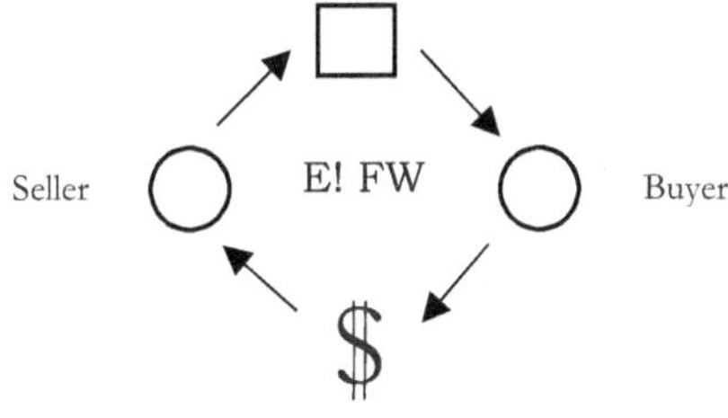

Figure 7: A WILLING BUYER TO A WILLING SELLER

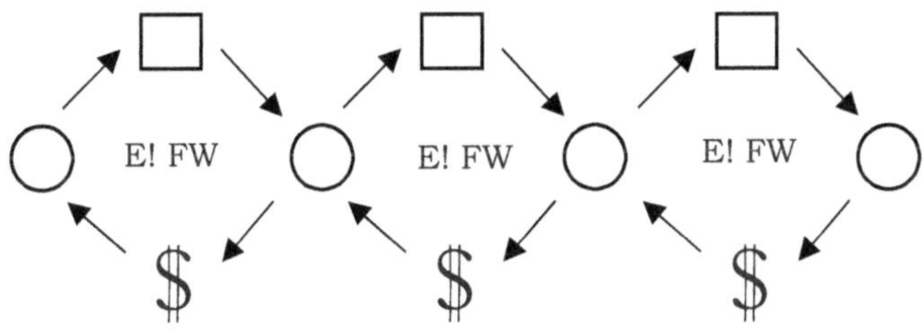

Figure 8: THE FREE MARKET SYSTEM

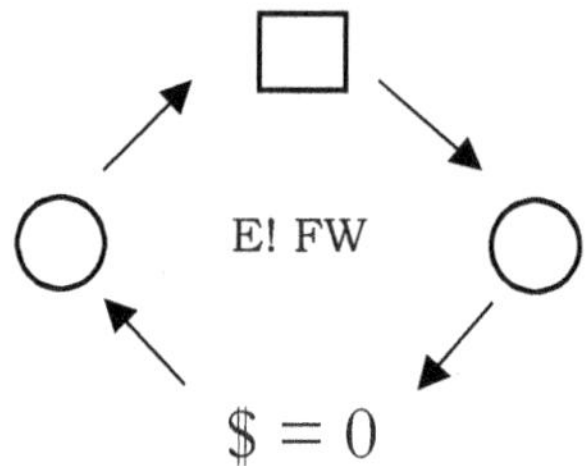

Figure 9: CHARITY

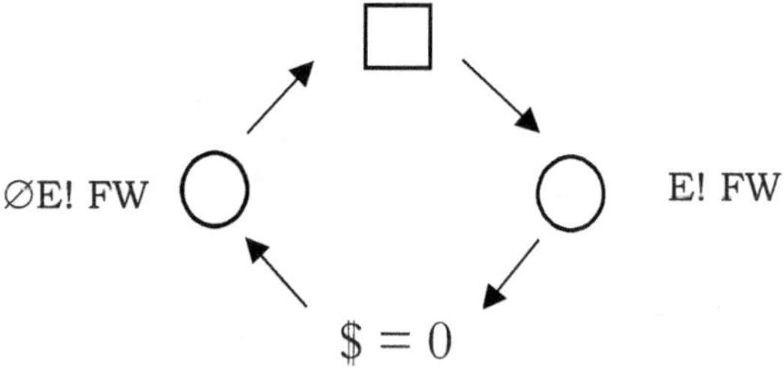

Figure 10: THEFT

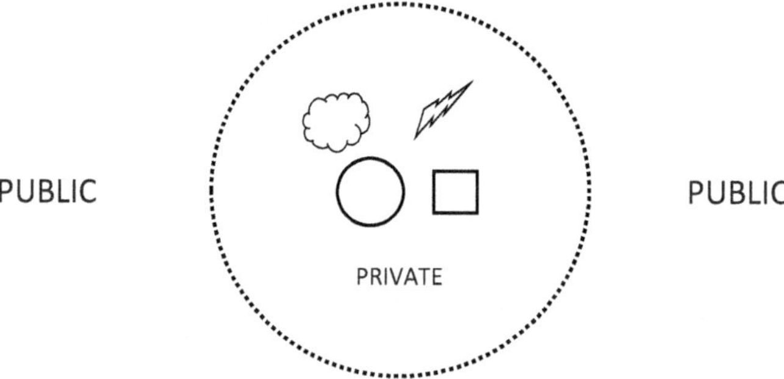

Figure 11: PRIVATE PROPERTY: Items within the circle are *private property*.

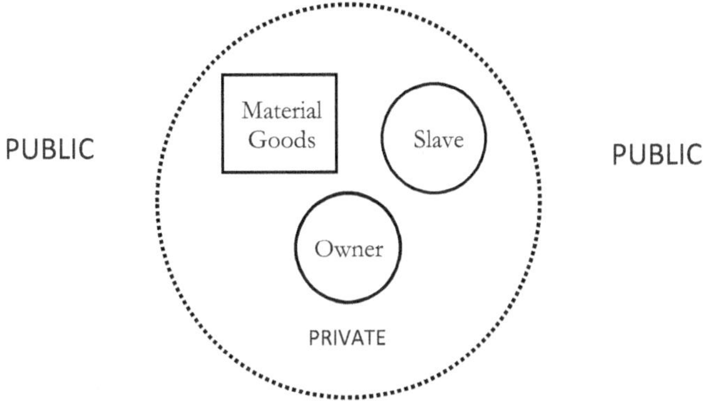

Figure 12: SLAVERY

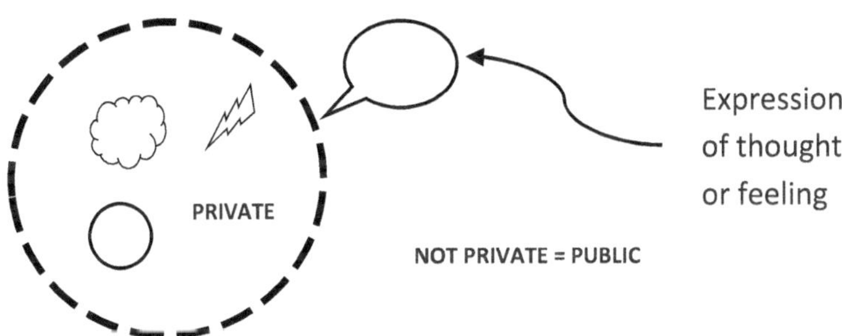

Figure 13: THE PUBLIC EXPRESSION OF THOUGHT AND FEELING

Figure 14: THE CREATION OF GOODS AND SERVICES

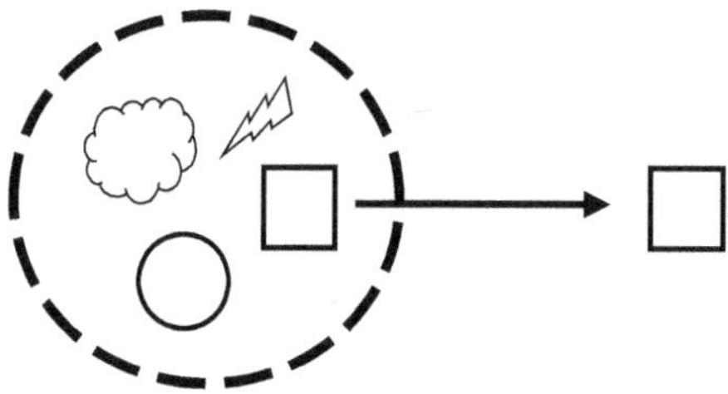

Figure 15: TRANSFER OF GOODS AND SERVICES FROM PRIVATE
TO PUBLIC REALM

□ = $

Figure 16: RELATIONSHIP BETWEEN GOODS AND SERVICES
AND VALUE

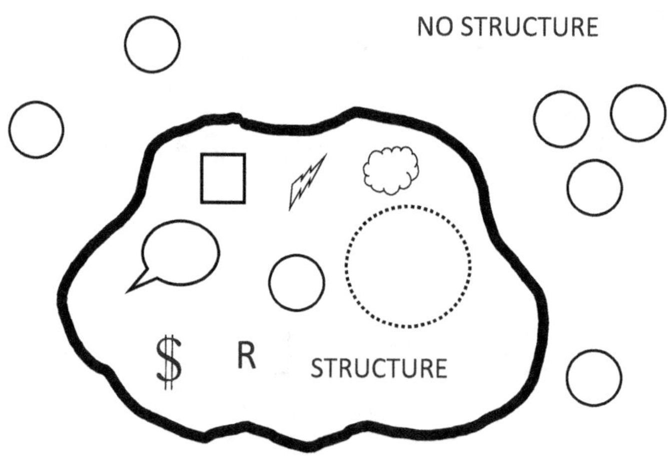

Figure 17: HUMAN SOCIAL STRUCTURE

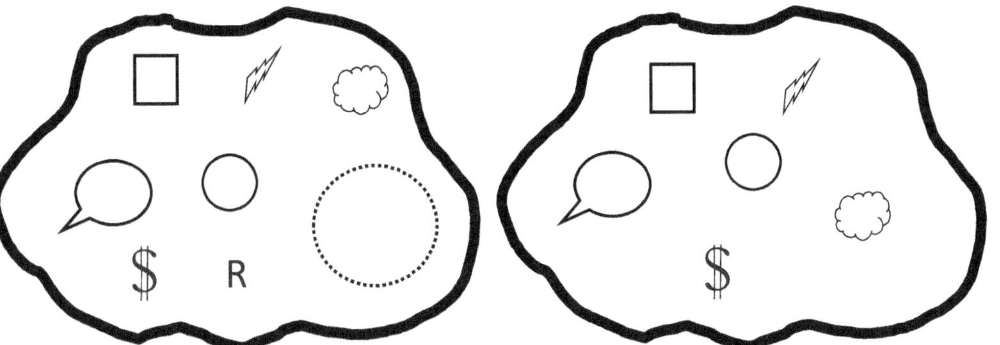

Figure 18: DIFFERENT HUMAN SOCIAL STRUCTURES

□ = motor vehicle

R = rules of the road

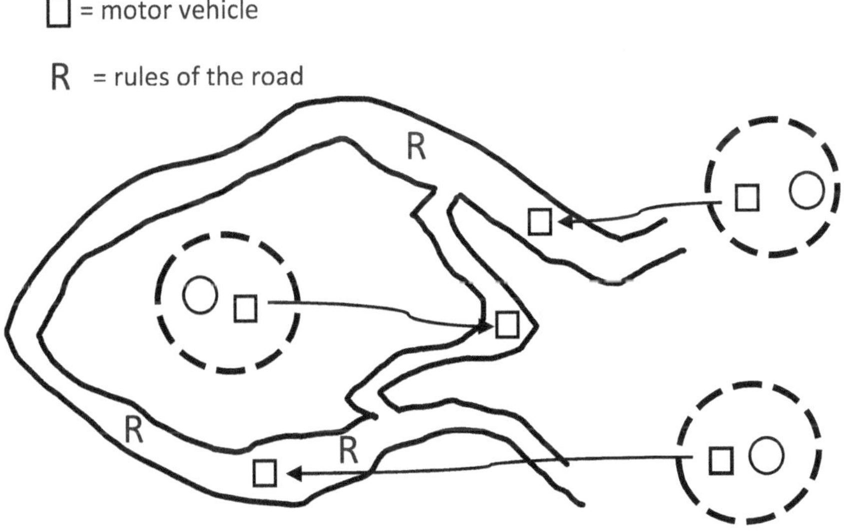

Figure 19: RULES OF THE ROAD FOR DRIVERS OF MOTOR VEHICLES

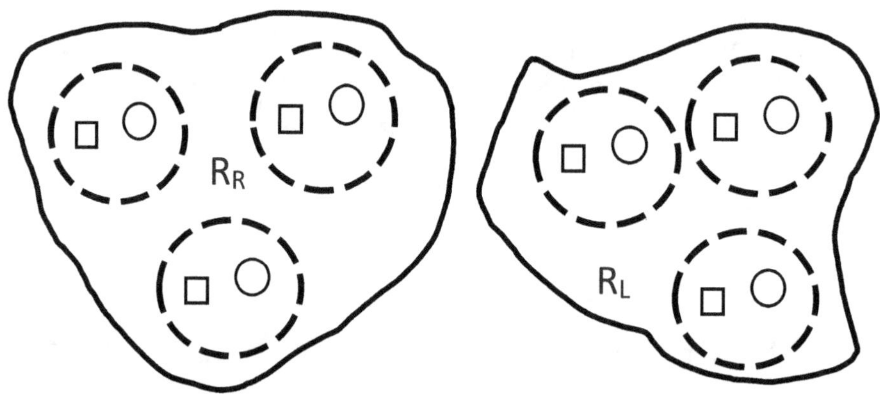

Figure 20: DIFFERENT RULES OF THE ROAD CREATE DISTINCT SOCIAL STRUCTURES

$$\overset{x}{\underset{N=1}{\Sigma}} R1 \quad > \quad \overset{x}{\underset{N=1}{\Sigma}} R2 \quad > \quad \overset{x}{\underset{N=1}{\Sigma}} R3$$

Figure 21: HIERARCHY OF SETS OF RULES

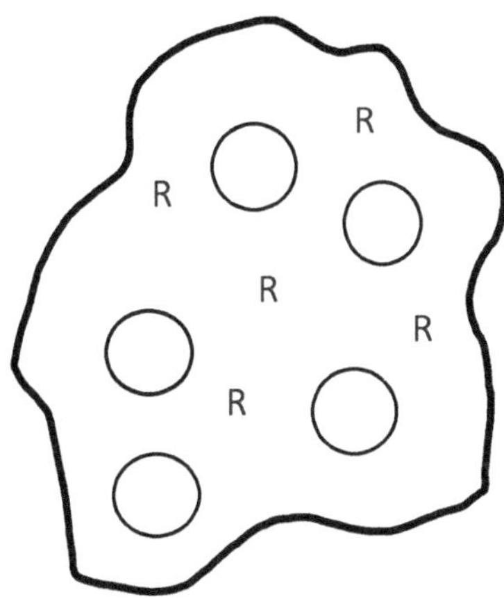

Figure 22: A GENERAL CONCEPT OF HUMAN SOCIAL STRUCTURE

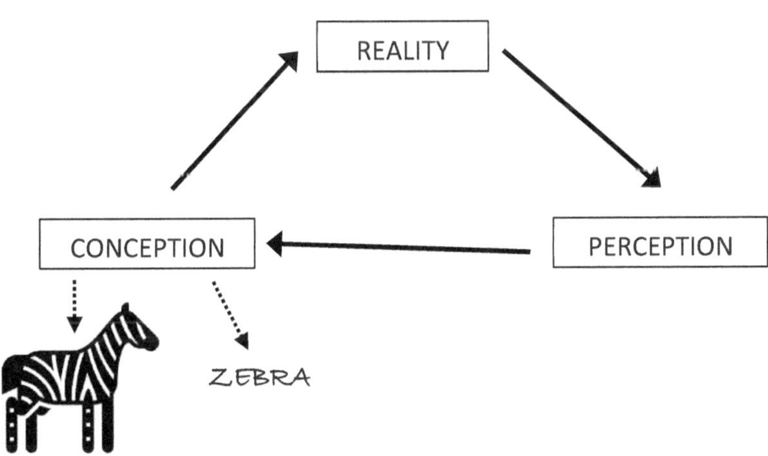

Figure 23: RELATIONSHIPS BETWEEN REALITY, PERCEPTION, AND CONCEPTION

GLOSSARY OF SOCIAL OBJECTS

OBJECT 1: An Individual human being

OBJECT 2: Human thought

OBJECT 3: Human feeling

OBJECT 4: A token of an individual human being

Begin   End

OBJECT 5: Time

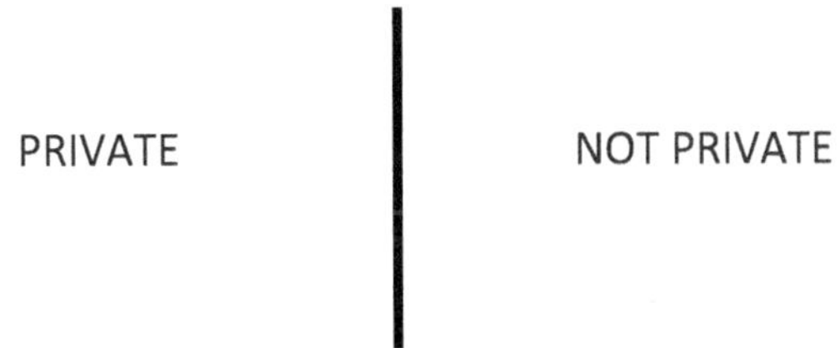

PRIVATE   NOT PRIVATE

OBJECT 6: The distinction between private and public

OBJECT 7: Private and public spaces

OBJECT 8: Expression of thought or feeling

OBJECT 9: Goods and Services

OBJECT 10: Value

=

OBJECT 11: Equal

R

OBJECT 12: Rules and Relationships

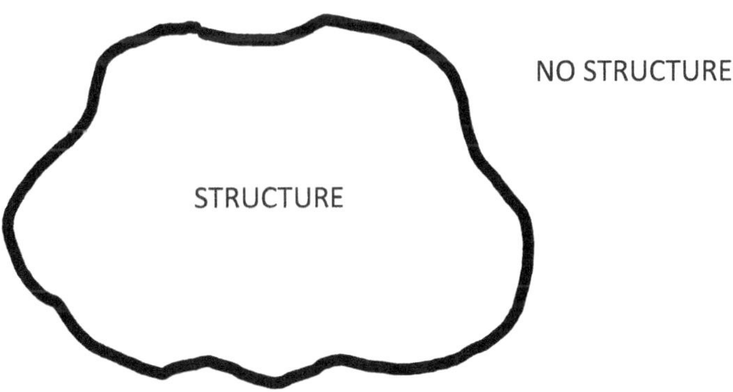

OBJECT 13: Border

$$\sum_{N=1}^{X} R$$

OBJECT 14: Set of Rules

ABOUT THE AUTHOR

Frank Cornelious Funk is a songsmith with a long-standing interest in the logical form of human society.

Other works by
FRANK CORNELIOUS FUNK

Books
iC, Part I
Songs in the Key of See

Music
Songs in the Key of See

Video
Mediocre Town 1ˢᵗ Edition

(Available on Amazon and You Tube)